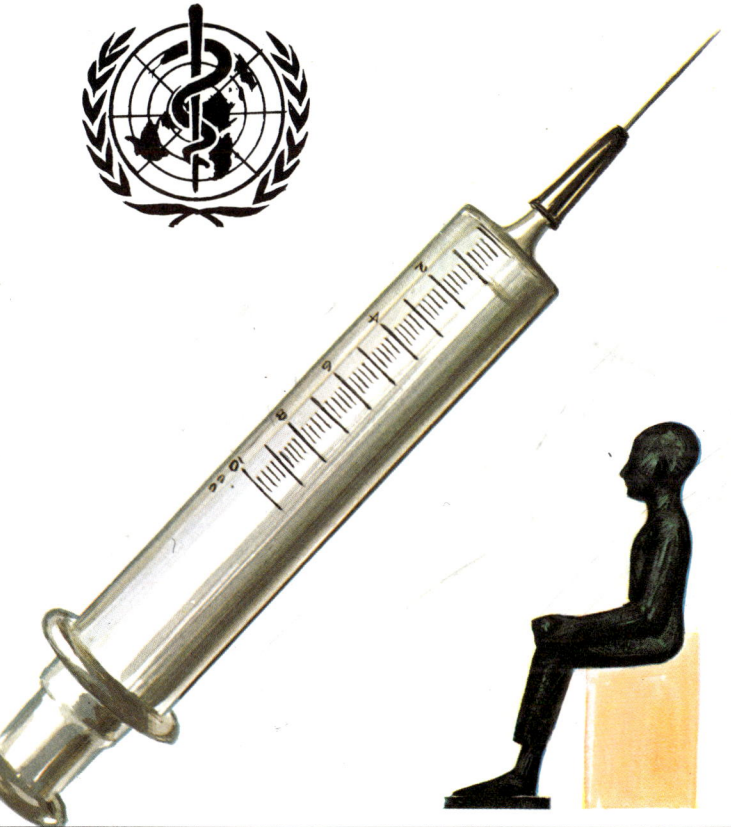

IN
HISTORY
SURGERY
AND MEDICINE

Authors:

David Smith and Derek Newton

Illustrated by Melvyn K. Powell

SCHOFIELD & SIMS LTD., HUDDERSFIELD

First impression 1972

© 1972 Schofield & Sims Ltd.

0 7217 1553 2
0 7217 1583 4 Net edition

Printed in England by W. S. Cowell Ltd, at the Butter Market, Ipswich.

Primitive Medicine

Primitive man lived in small communities so there was less danger of infection, but, being nomadic people, only the fittest survived. By trial and error they learned which plants healed and which were poisonous. This knowledge was usually remembered by one member of the tribe and he became the medicine-man or witch-doctor. He handed down his knowledge to his son. Sometimes a drug would heal one person but not another so the witch-doctor blamed his failures on evil spirits. Thus, medicine became connected with magic. Besides giving medicine, the doctor cast a spell to fight the evil spirits.

The primitive doctor performed crude surgical operations with a stone knife, and skulls have been found with holes cut out of them, probably to release evil spirits. Some skeletons have been unearthed showing that the cavity had been reduced in size by bone growth. This meant that the person under treatment had lived on after the operation. Other bones found show fractures which had healed and these are evidence of some knowledge of bone-setting.

Assyria and Babylon

The first civilisation to leave written medical records was that in Mesopotamia, where many wax tablets have been found with prescriptions for medicines written on them, dating back to 3000 B.C.

In primitive times sick people were taken to the market place where other people who had suffered from the same disease could meet them and advise them what to do. Lepers were expelled from the towns to prevent the spreading of the disease.

Slowly a class of 'priest-physicians' grew up. Their medicine was a mixture of knowledge of drugs and magic. There were two kinds of doctors: 'Ashipu', who used medicines for internal disorders, and 'Asu', who were surgeons and dealt with external wounds and sores.

The dosage of drugs, especially dangerous ones like opium and belladonna, was carefully controlled. Drugs were first tried out on slaves to find the correct dosage.

The Code of Hammurabi listed the fees which a surgeon could charge, and it also stated the punishment if a patient died.

Sick people receiving advice

3

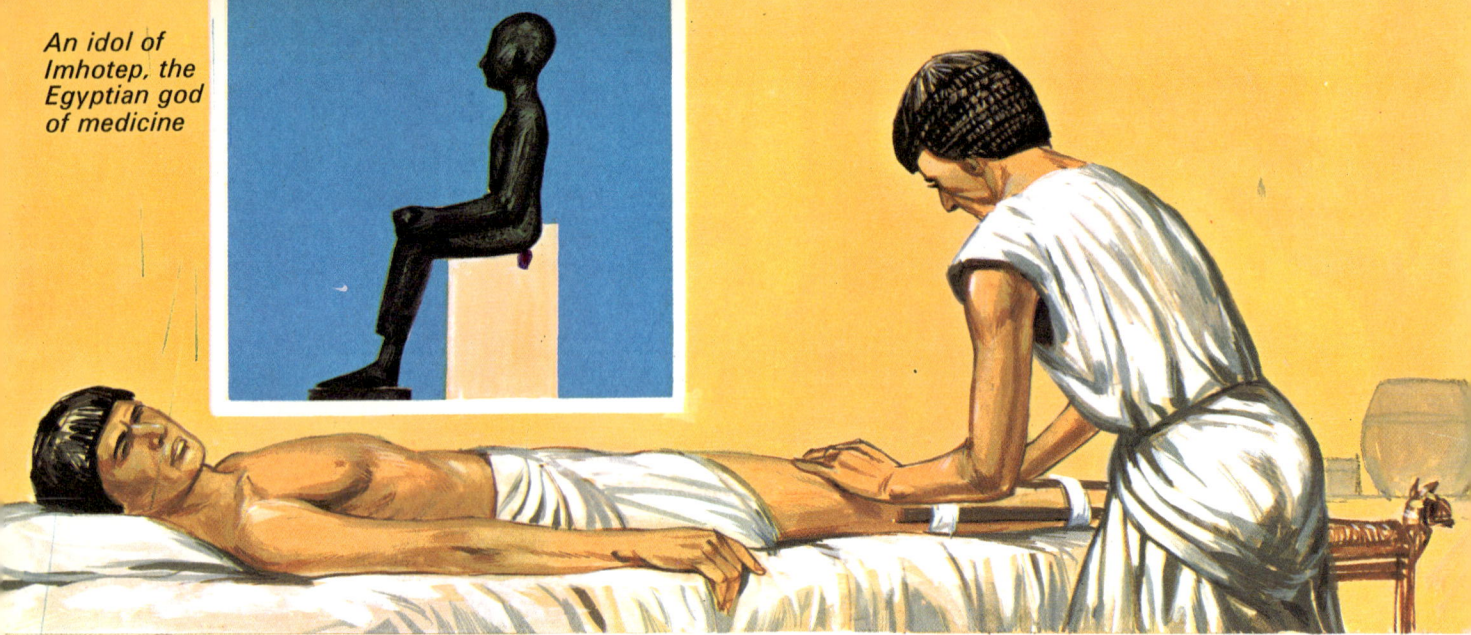

An idol of Imhotep, the Egyptian god of medicine

An Egyptian doctor putting a broken leg in splints

Ancient Egypt

Magic was still used along with medicine. The priests and sorcerers impressed the patients by the spells they cast as well as by the medicine they gave. Medicines contained revolting ingredients such as snake fat, for the Egyptians believed that the nastier a medicine tasted, the more effective it was. They had both pills and liquid medicines. A roll of papyrus, known as the 'Ebers Papyrus', has been found with over nine hundred names of medicines written on it.

The Egyptians embalmed the dead and preserved their bodies. To do this they removed the internal organs, thus gaining important knowledge of how the body worked.

Specialists appeared who dealt with sickness in one part of the body only. They performed operations, prescribed drugs and knew how to treat dislocations and put splints and plaster on broken limbs.

The Egyptians were also aware of the importance of hygiene and knew the value of good sanitation and clean water.

Ancient Greece

The Greeks had temples of healing dedicated to Asclepius, the god of healing. Here, priests saw that the patients had a sensible diet, rest, and fresh air. The priests kept sacred snakes and a snake or serpent coiled round a staff is still the symbol of medicine.

Hippocrates is remembered as the greatest of the Greek doctors. He firmly believed that every disease had a natural cause, and he preached careful observation of the patient to help diagnose symptoms. The 'Hippocratic Oath', named after him, gave the medical profession a sense of duty to mankind which it never lost. Many students still take the Oath. They swear to respect their patients, do all they can to help them, and keep secret anything which is told to them.

Hippocrates taught that the body was made up of four elements: blood, phlegm, yellow bile, and black bile. It was the doctor's duty to see that a balance of these 'humours' was kept.

The Greeks had a wide knowledge of drugs. Dioscorides wrote five books on drugs, with drawings of plants and advice on how to use the medicines.

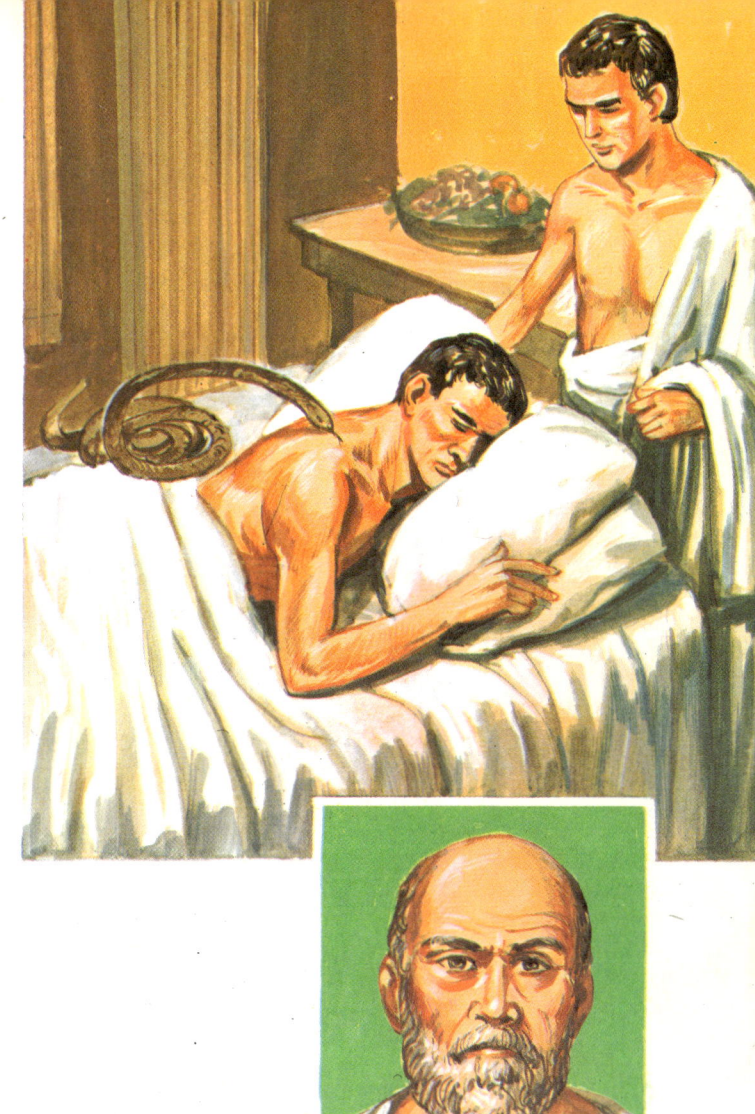

Hippocrates

5

Ancient Rome

The Romans considered the medical profession to be only fit for slaves. Nevertheless, the greatest doctor of the Ancient World, after Hippocrates, was one of those despised slaves, a Greek called Galen.

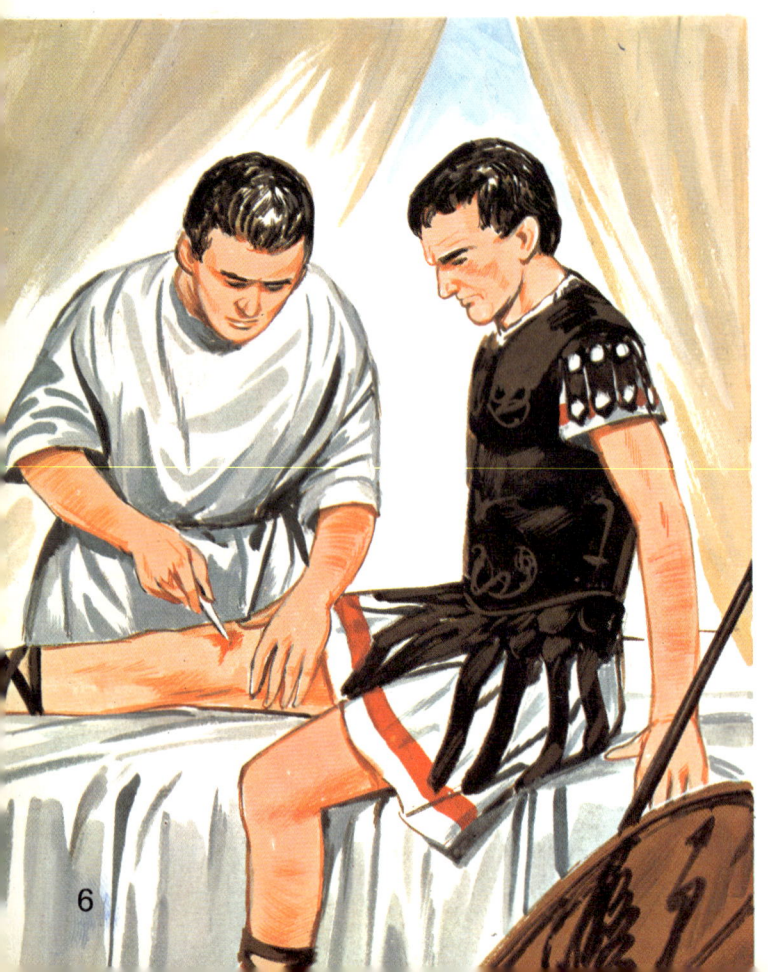

Galen's ideas influenced medicine for hundreds of years and he was physician to five Roman Emperors.

Julius Caesar granted Roman citizenship to Greek doctors and Augustus excused them from paying taxes.

During the Christian Era of the Empire doctors were appointed to take care of the poor.

Hospitals

The Roman army had surgeons. In A.D. 14 Augustus began a military medical service. By the fourth century hospitals were built in all military camps.

The gladiatorial schools, too, had hospitals, while each large house had a room as a hospital for the sick slaves.

In 398 Fabiola built in Rome the first free public hospital. One of the first medical schools for doctors was founded at Salerno in Italy about the year 400.

Hygiene and Health

The Romans had excellent sanitary arrangements for their time. Markets were supervised and the sale of food controlled. Each large city had underground sewers, aqueducts to bring fresh water, public and private baths, and flush lavatories.

China

About 3000 B.C. the people of Ancient China, too, had priest-physicians, but gradually doctors became a separate profession. *The Canon of Internal Medicine* was a Chinese book which provided a sound knowledge of anatomy, physiology, and a knowledge of the pulse and the circulation of the blood. The Chinese had physicians, surgeons and dieticians.

India

About the year 1600 B.C. sacred books of medicine, called the *Reg Vedas*, were written. The Indians had a knowledge of plastic surgery, skin-grafting, and eye operations. The kings had hospitals built as gifts to the people.

Arabian Medicine

There was also a knowledge of medicine in the East, mainly among the Arabs.

They had alchemists who knew some chemistry. They were also able to distil and make crystals, and purify drugs.

Anald of Villanova used alcohol to extract drugs from herbs. A Persian doctor, Rhazes, discovered the difference between measles and smallpox. Avicenna, another

An illustration from the cover of 'The Canon of Medicine'

famous Persian doctor, wrote a book of medicine called *The Canon of Medicine* which was used by doctors until the sixteenth century.

The Dark Ages

Saxons

With the collapse of the Roman Empire in the fifth century, medical knowledge went into a decline, but a little learning was spread among the monasteries and abbeys. Magic reappeared in the treatment of illness. The Saxons thought disease was caused by worms or elves! Here was their remedy for toothache: 'Take a candle of mutton fat mingled with the seed of sea holly. Burn it close to the tooth until the worms fall out.' They believed charms worn round the neck prevented illness. 'ABRACADABRA' was a magic word which was used as a spell by the Saxons. A book of Saxon spells and prescriptions called the *Lacnunga* has been found. The Saxons believed there was poison in the air and they had spells to ward off flying venom. Their doctors were called 'leeches', because they put leeches on a sore spot to relieve the pain by sucking blood.

A leech

The Coming of Christianity

It was a Christian duty to take care of the sick. Even though the sick had to be nursed, the Church taught that sickness was God's punishment. St. Bernard of Clairvaux said it was sinful to buy drugs, consult physicians, or take medicines. Yet each monastery had an infirmary for the sick monks, another for the lay brothers, and a 'hospice' where the poor could rest and be cared for.

The monks cultivated herb gardens, made up mixtures of simple drugs, and did simple surgery. The drugs were stored in a 'pharmacy'.

Some priests acted as physicians outside the monasteries. A monk, Baldwin, became physician to Edward the Confessor, and he also treated William the Conqueror.

There was still, however, a belief in mystery and magic. Saints were supposed to have the power to heal. Each saint was thought to have power over one part of the human body, and pilgrims visited their shrines to be cured. Holy relics, such as a fragment of Christ's manger, were believed to have healing properties.

Pilgrims visit a shrine, seeking a cure

9

The Middle Ages

As more people lived in towns a series of plagues swept through Western civilisation. From the eleventh century to the thirteenth century leprosy was a loathsome disease. By the thirteenth century there were about 19 000 leper houses. Even so, lepers still roamed the countryside carrying a clapper or rattle, and a bell to warn unwary travellers. Some town authorities provided hospitals. There were infirmaries for cripples, the blind, and those who were mentally sick. St. Bartholomew's Hospital which was once a priory was founded in 1123 by Rahere, a minstrel, who later became a monk. St. Thomas's and St. Mary of Bethlehem hospitals in London were founded at about the same time but there was little regular nursing. Usually the healthier inmates looked after the others. Sometimes there were as many as six patients in one bed!

Patients being bled

Trained Doctors

It was obvious that trained doctors were necessary. Medical schools were set up in the thirteenth century at Paris, Cologne, Padua and Bologna, as well as the one at Salerno. The Holy Roman Emperor Frederick II decided that each student should pass an examination before he could call himself 'Doctor'. It is believed that the first qualified doctors date from 1221. Each student had five years' training, followed by a year's apprenticeship. King Henry V of England ordered that all doctors should have a university degree from Oxford or Cambridge.

Medical knowledge was scanty and little was known about the human body. The cutting up of corpses to find out more about the body was frowned upon. Doctors continued to study the books of Hippocrates, Galen and Avicenna. Some medicines contained many drugs in the hope that one of them would cure the illness. 'Bleeding' was the most common treatment.

Drugs and Medicines

Drugs in the Middle Ages were sold by shopkeepers, who were called 'spicers' or 'pepperers' because they imported spices like pepper, as well as drugs and ingredients for medicines. Some ingredients were difficult to obtain and so herbs which could be grown in this country were tried. Books called 'herbals' were written containing prescriptions for medicines made up from the more easily-obtained drugs.

Apothecaries

Medicines were dispensed by apothecaries. During the early part of the Middle Ages apothecaries travelled the country selling poisons, drugs and love potions, but by 1400 many apothecaries were conducting their business from shops in the towns. They prepared their medicines in a room at the back of the shop. Pills were rolled on tiles, and so the apothecary used a tile as his trade sign. A medicine made from one herb or drug was called a 'simple', while one made up of more than a single ingredient was called a 'compound'. Some compounds had as many as sixty-three ingredients. These were called 'theriacs'.

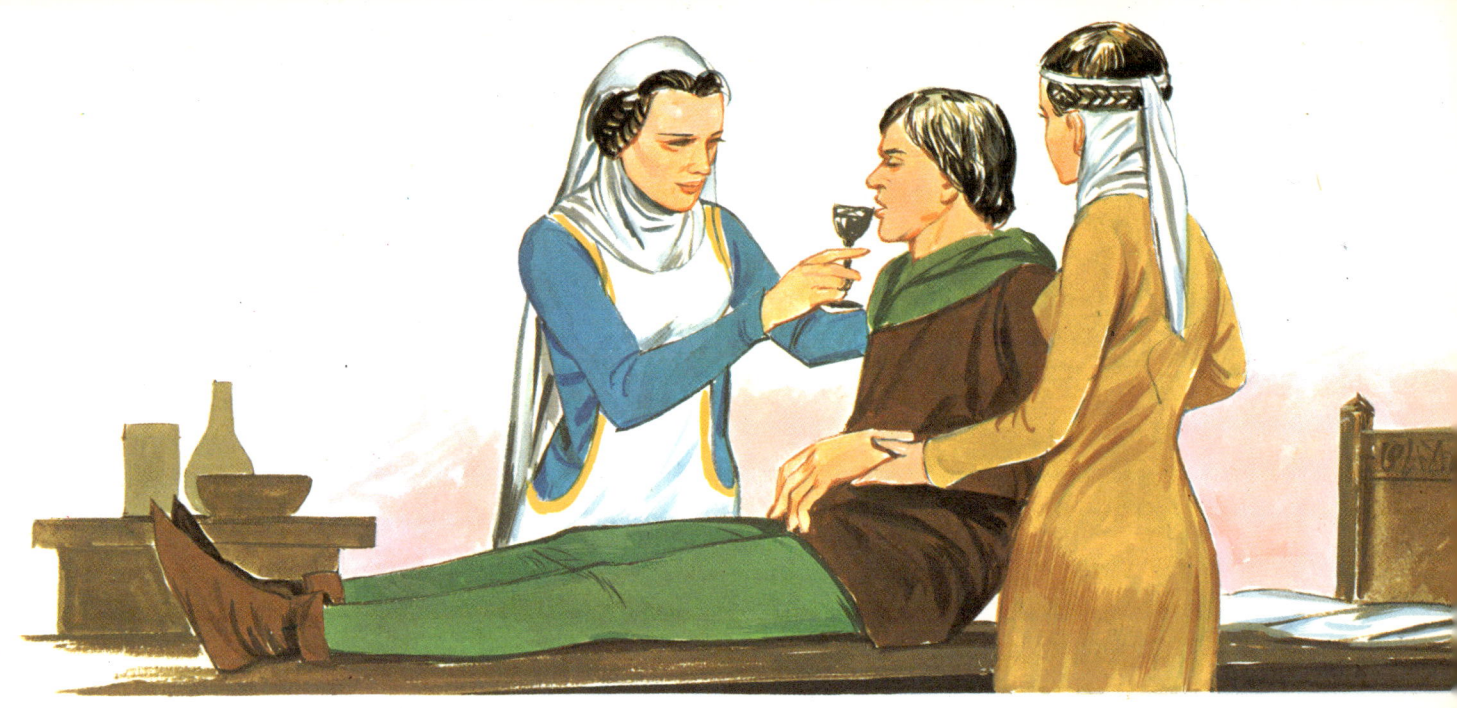

Some ingredients came from plants. Apothecaries dried herbs and leaves and stored them in jars so that they would be available all the year round. Other ingredients were obtained from animals. Powdered cuttlefish, for example, was used for indigestion.

Home Nursing

Much nursing in the country districts was carried on in the home. The wife of the lord of the manor ministered to the poor, and also to the sick people in her household. A herbal was available in almost every large home, and girls were taught simple medicine and surgery, and how to deal with wounds.

Their knowledge was scanty, however. During outbreaks of the plague called the 'Black Death', it was thought that keeping a billy-goat in the house kept the air sweet. It was also believed that if warm, new bread was put in the mouth of a sick person it would absorb the poison.

Tudors and Stuarts

The invention of printing by Gutenberg helped people to obtain more knowledge from books on medicine. Students had a wider choice of authors and illustrations. Artists, like Leonardo da Vinci, Michelangelo, Raphael and Dürer, studied bones and dead bodies so that their paintings were more realistic. Some doctors encouraged students to study people rather than books. Paracelsus, a Swiss alchemist, made a public bonfire of certain Ancient Greek and Latin medical books.

Andreas Vesalius

More and more doctors began to dissect dead bodies. In 1543 Andreas Vesalius published his book *The Workings of the Human Body*. Vesalius had trained in Paris. He took the bodies of highwaymen and robbers which were hanging from the gibbets, in order to dissect them and find out more about the body. When only twenty-four he became Professor of Anatomy at Padua, Italy. By his example, he changed teaching methods for medical students.

*A copy of an illustration
from 'The Workings of the Human Body'*

William Harvey

William Harvey

An English doctor, William Harvey, who was on the staff of St. Bartholomew's Hospital, published a book in 1628 called *Concerning the Motion of the Heart and Blood*. In this book he proved that the heart worked like a pump which caused the blood to circulate through the arteries, back along the veins, through the lungs, and back into the heart again. He showed that there were valves in the heart and veins which allowed the blood to flow in only one direction.

Experiments with Air

Robert Boyle, Joseph Priestley and Antoine Lavoisier experimented with air and found that the body used oxygen. They also proved that a man who was working needed more oxygen than one who was resting.

Lavoisier experimenting

Increased Medical Knowledge

A Dutchman, Van Leeuwenhoek, ground lenses for microscopes. When he put some saliva from his mouth under his microscope he saw that it was alive with what he called 'little animals'. These were the first 'micro-organisms' to be seen.

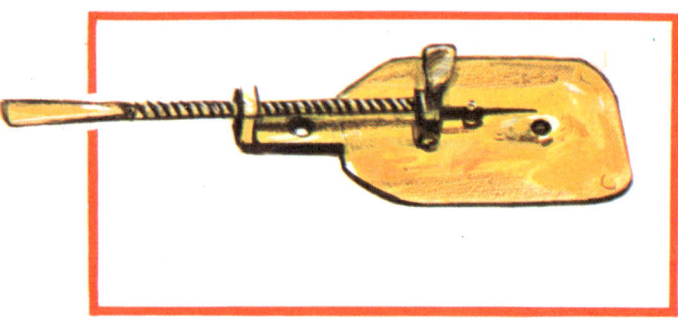

Leeuwenhoek's microscope

Sanctorius, an Italian, invented a clinical thermometer for taking a person's temperature.

A blood transfusion from one dog to another was successfully carried out.

'Quinine', a drug which helped to cure malaria, was brought back by sailors from South America.

Medical books were now written in English. A medical dictionary, *The Breviarie of Health*, was published by Andrew Boorde in 1547.

A plague doctor in his bird-like helmet

Civil Control of Hospitals

After the dissolution of the monasteries by Henry VIII many hospitals were neglected or closed. In 1547 the City of London obtained permission from Edward VI to take over St. Bartholomew's, St. Thomas's, Bridewell, and St. Mary of Bethlehem Hospital. This was the beginning of civil control of hospitals, and of lay nursing, that is, nursing not done by monks or nuns.

For the next three hundred years there was no regular, trained nursing staff, though the titles 'Matron' and 'Sister' were retained.

Quarantine

During the fourteenth century Venice had its own public health department. It became the practice for all new arrivals from a plague area to be isolated for forty days. This quarantine could check the spread of disease. Other towns soon copied this example.

During the seventeenth century, houses which contained plague victims were isolated and the doors marked to warn other people. Watchmen were put on guard outside to see that no one left the building.

Plague doctors realised the dangers of infection. They wore long robes and gauntlets and tried to feel a patient's pulse by using a 'wand'. On their heads they wore a helmet with a bird-like beak which held spices to keep out the bad air.

Magic

Magic was still associated with medicine, even in the sixteenth and seventeenth centuries. Women who were suspected of being witches were hunted down and burned.

A disease called 'scrofula' was known as 'King's Evil' because it was believed that the touch of a king could cure it. It had been known since the time of Edward the Confessor and the cure was still believed in during the seventeenth century.

The touch of the king was believed to cure King's Evil

17

Doctors

It was not necessary to be qualified to treat the sick. There were few qualified doctors so anyone who knew anything about medicine was allowed to practise. The lady of the manor still helped with the sick, and every village had its wise old woman with a knowledge of herbs.

Unqualified doctors called 'quacks' made up medicines, sold them at fairs and markets, and then quickly moved on to another district.

Henry VIII granted a Royal Charter to physicians and surgeons which gave them special privileges. The English College of Physicians was founded in Henry VIII's reign.

The apothecaries received a Royal Charter from James I in 1617. This said that every apothecary had to undergo a seven years' apprenticeship.

Medical Treatment

The physicians, apothecaries, and chemists worked together. The physicians ordered the medicine from the apothecaries who had herbs and animal and vegetable drugs in their pharmacies. They bought drugs such as sulphur, mercury, and arsenic from the chemists.

Each member of the group was jealous of the others. Physicians accused apothecaries of using cheap drugs, and apothecaries accused chemists of supplying impure drugs.

A doctor collecting medicine from the apothecary

Apothecaries become Doctors

The apothecaries began to attend to the sick who could not afford the doctors' fees, and gradually they took on more and more of the doctors' work. In this way they became doctors. By 1700 they had the rights by law to examine patients and prescribe treatment. The chemists started to dispense drugs and their stores began to look more like a chemist's shop as we know it today.

Surgeons

Surgery was carried out by doctor-surgeons and barber-surgeons.

The barber-surgeons trimmed beards, cut hair, drew teeth, lanced boils, and even performed amputations.

The doctor-surgeons resented their work and would not allow barber-surgeons to visit the sick in hospital.

During the thirteenth century Henry de Mondeville and a few others established surgery as a profession in its own right. They took medical degrees and were called 'Surgeons of the Long Robe'.

Army Surgeons

When gunpowder began to be used in warfare early in the fourteenth century, surgeons were in great demand in the army. Wounds were treated with boiling oil and pitch. It was Ambroise Paré, a French surgeon, who first used soothing ointments and clean bandages for wounds.

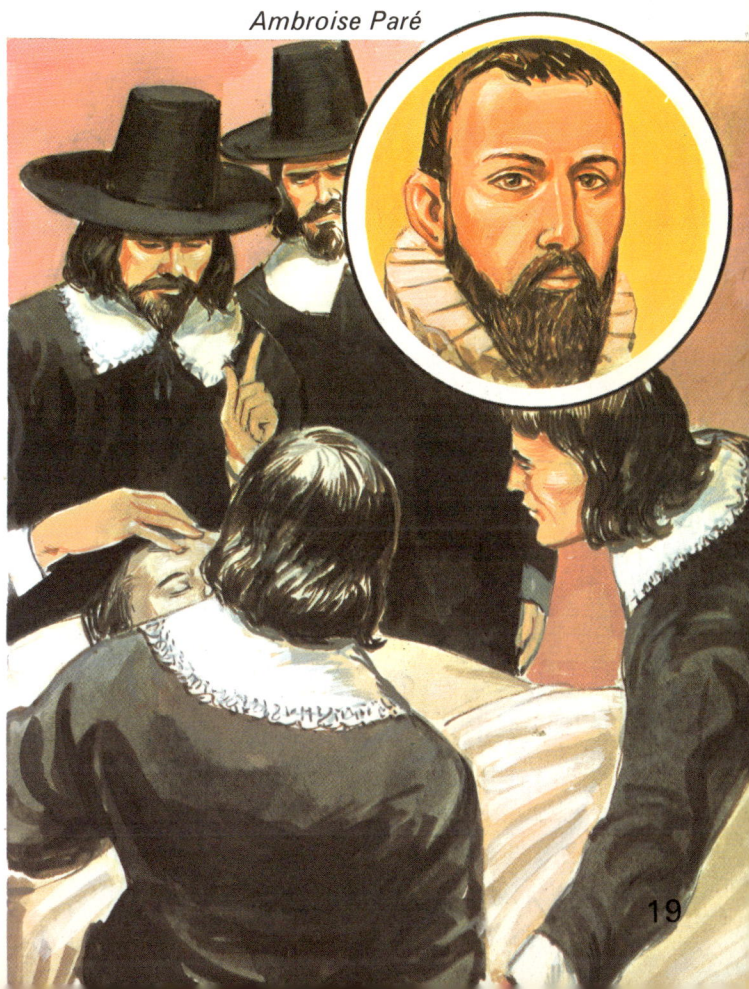

Ambroise Paré

Surgeons giving an anatomy lesson to students

19

Patients consulting
a quack

Georgian Times

By 1800 most districts had doctors, but many of them were quacks. Many doctors were held in contempt, as there seemed to be so little they could do to heal people. Some doctors believed in rest and a careful diet, and others believed in drugs like the 'theriac' and pills the size of grapes.

The eighteenth century saw some improvement in the treatment of disease.

Smallpox

During the seventeenth century smallpox was a scourge to health and at least half the people in Britain were pockmarked.

On 1st April 1717 Lady Mary Wortley Montagu wrote from Constantinople describing how people there were injected with a dose of smallpox. Those who were injected in this way had a mild attack of the disease, but soon recovered.

This practice of immunising against smallpox had been carried on in the East for centuries. The Chinese used to soak a piece of cotton-wool in the pus of a smallpox sore and then put it up the nose of the patient. This method was not entirely successful as a dangerous dose could still be given.

Edward Jenner

It was Edward Jenner, an English doctor, who discovered a safe way to immunise against smallpox.

People who had a great deal to do with cows caught a mild disease called cowpox. These people never caught smallpox. On the 14th May 1796 Edward Jenner took some pus from a cowpox sore on the hand of a milkmaid, Sarah Nelmes, and injected it into the arm of James Phipps, an eight-year-old boy. Later he inoculated the boy with smallpox. The boy did not catch the disease. The harmless cowpox germs had caused the body to make germ-fighters, called 'antibodies', which killed the smallpox germs. Jenner's work was at first ignored but in 1799 the idea was tried in Austria. It was so successful that the value of Jenner's discovery was at last realised and Parliament granted him the sum of £10,000. A few years later they gave him a further grant of money.

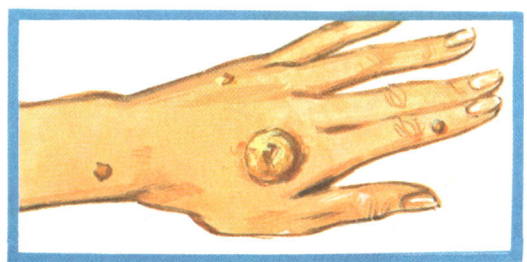

Cowpox sores

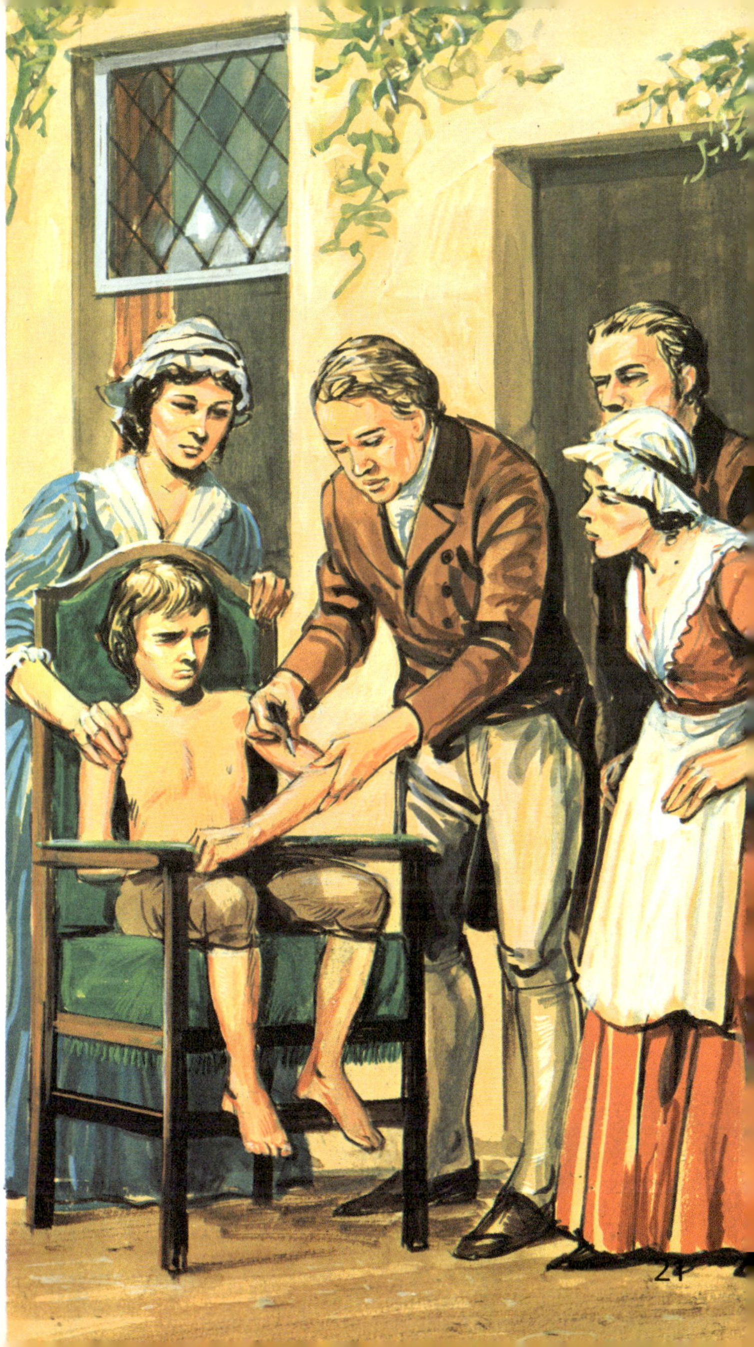

*Edward Jenner
immunising
James Phipps*

Scurvy

The fight against disease was strengthened when it was realised that people needed a balanced diet. For years sailors had suffered from a disease called 'scurvy'. At sea the sailors existed on hard biscuits and salt meat, a diet lacking in vitamins. As early as 1535 Jacques Cartier, the French explorer, found that the natives of North America could cure his sailors of scurvy with a potion of spruce tree needles.

It was also noticed that the poorer people suffered from scurvy in winter but in summer the fresh vegetables they ate kept the scurvy away.

In 1600 James Lancaster suggested that eating fresh lemons and oranges would cure scurvy. The East India Company began to issue sailors with a ration of lemon juice.

James Lind, a doctor at Portsmouth Naval Hospital, studied the subject. In 1753 he published his findings and suggested a ration of fresh fruit.

In the 1770s this suggestion was acted on by Captain Cook, and on a three years' voyage not one man died of scurvy. By 1804 a ration of lemon juice was regularly issued to sailors on many ships.

Mental Illness

For centuries it was believed that people who were mentally ill were possessed by devils. Those who were well-to-do could go to private asylums, but most insane people were kept in general hospitals or in one of the few public asylums like St. Mary of Bethlehem Hospital, better known as Bedlam, in London.

Some mental patients were kept chained up, and the usual treatment was bleeding, starving, whipping or shock treatment.

Many people regarded a visit to an asylum as an enjoyable day's outing, as it gave them a chance to laugh at the strange behaviour of the inmates.

This gruesome practice was stopped at St. Luke's Hospital in London in 1751. After 1770 no visitors were allowed at Bedlam without a special pass, and after 1774 visiting merely for viewing was forbidden in all mental hospitals.

In 1792 William Tuke founded the York Retreat for thirty mental patients. He treated the inmates with kindness and found simple jobs for them to do.

In 1793 Philippe Pinel, at the Bicêtre Hospital in Paris, removed the chains from his patients.

There was an enquiry into asylums in 1815 to see what could be done to provide real help for the patients.

Inside Bedlam

Pinel removing the chains

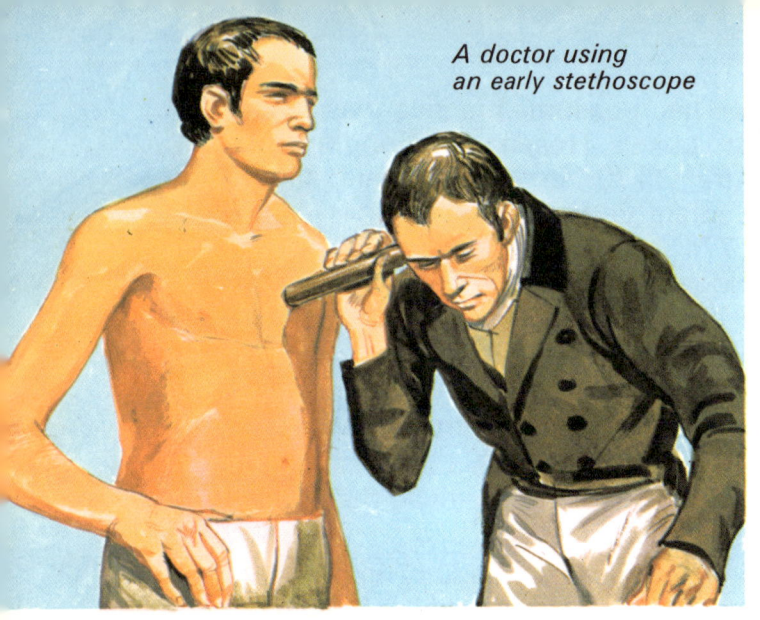

A doctor using an early stethoscope

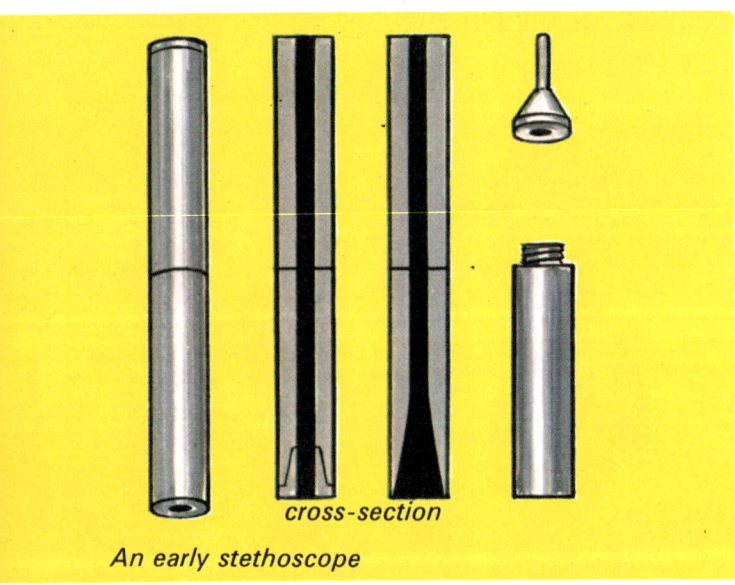

cross-section

An early stethoscope

Improved Diagnosis

Leopold Auenbrugger, an Austrian, sought a better method of finding out more accurately the type of disease from which a patient was suffering.

His aid to diagnosis was called 'percussion'. He would tap the chest with his knuckle and listen carefully to the kind of sound this produced. He believed this method would help doctors to spot the cause of the trouble. His idea gained little support at the time, but later it was used by Napoleon's doctor, Corvisart.

In 1816 René Laënnec devised a stethoscope. He rolled up a sheaf of paper, placed it over a sick person's heart and found that he could hear the heartbeat more clearly. One of the earliest stethoscopes, a simple, hollow, wooden tube, was introduced into England by John Elliotson.

An American army surgeon, William Beaumont, gained fame for his studies of the process of digestion. He treated a trapper who had a gunshot wound in the stomach. The wound did not heal over and so the lining of the stomach was visible. Beaumont fed him different types of food to find out the length of time required to digest each type. From his experiments Beaumont was able to show how the digestive system worked.

Manchester
Royal Infirmary

Hospitals

The eighteenth century was an age of great hospital building. London Hospital was opened in 1740, Middlesex Hospital in 1745, Liverpool Royal in 1749, and Manchester Royal in 1753. From 1700–1835 more than one hundred and fifty hospitals were built in Britain. Many were voluntary hospitals – that is, they were built with money given by kind-hearted people – and they were maintained by charity. Patients paid what they could afford for their treatment. Doctors usually gave their services free.

Conditions in the hospitals were not good as there were no properly-trained nurses. The wards were often dirty and disease spread quickly. Sometimes several patients shared one bed. Attempts were made to improve the many defects. Leeds Infirmary in Yorkshire, was known as an exceptionally good hospital.

Local authorities were obliged to provide work-houses. These were intended for those in great need but soon they had wards for the feeble, old and infirm. The healthier inmates looked after the less able.

Curing Disease

Until the middle of the nineteenth century very little was known about germs. People saw no link between disease and dirt. Van Leeuwenhoek's discovery of 'little animals' had been almost forgotten and there was still little effective treatment for disease, apart from Jenner's method of vaccination.

Slowly, men began to appreciate the link between dirt and disease. In 1854 Dr. John Snow noticed during a cholera epidemic in London that over five hundred people died in one district, and they had all drunk water from the same pump. Dr. Snow realised there must be germs in the water so he had the pump turned off and the death rate fell.

Louis Pasteur

Louis Pasteur contributed most to man's knowledge of germs. During his experiments in 1857, when he was observing the fermenting of beet-sugar, he discovered that the fermenting process was caused by living organisms and that it was germs in the air which caused the beet-sugar to go bad. In 1865 he devised a method of killing germs in milk by using heat. This method, which is still used, is called 'pasteurization'.

Louis Pasteur

Robert Koch

During his experiments in 1879 Pasteur injected some chicken cholera germs, which he had stored, into chickens. Although the chickens caught the disease they recovered and were then immune to the disease. Pasteur realised that the germs he had stored had become weaker, and that he had stumbled upon a new way of vaccination against sickness.

A German scientist, Robert Koch, had also done valuable work to increase man's knowledge of germs. Building on Koch's work, Pasteur produced a vaccine to immunise people against anthrax.

Within four years vaccines were available for chicken cholera, anthrax, and rabies. Later, there were vaccines for cholera, typhoid and yellow fever. Between 1879 and 1900 the germs of at least twenty-one diseases were discovered.

In 1898 Sir Ronald Ross made the important discovery that malaria was caused by the bite of a type of mosquito, and plans were made to drain or spray with disinfectant the swamps where the mosquitoes bred.

Sir Ronald Ross

Spraying the swamps with disinfectant

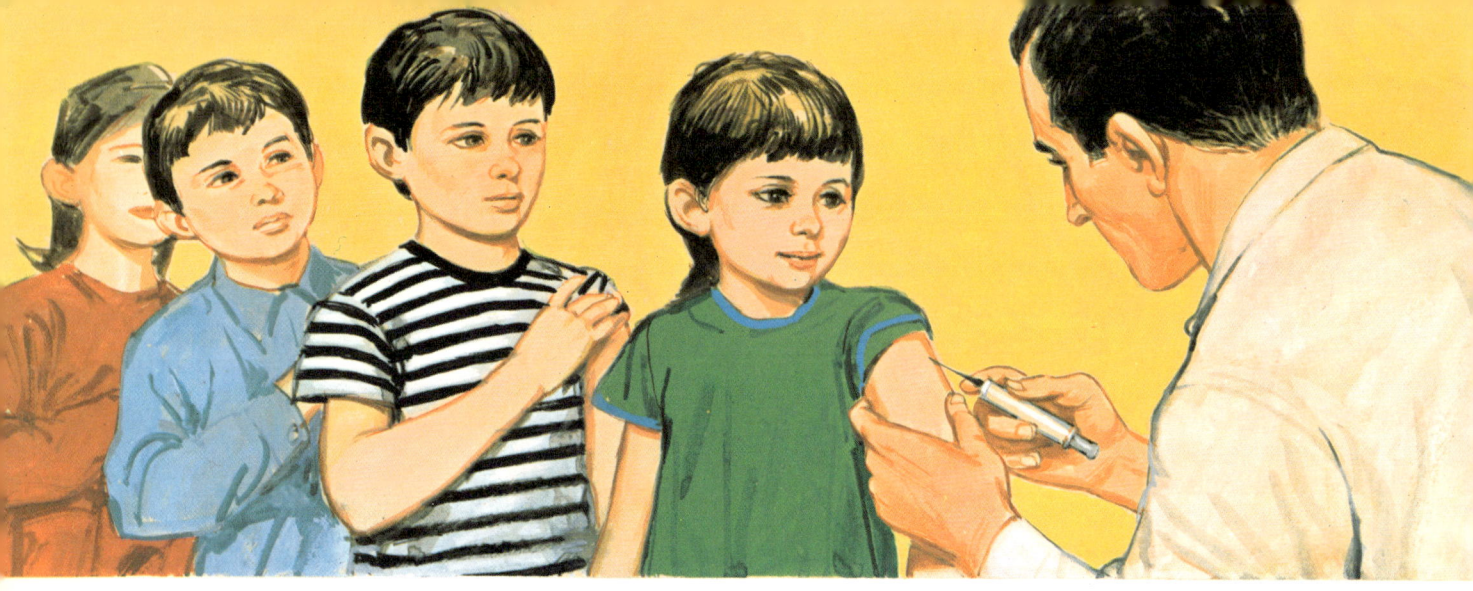

Other scientists discovered that the injection of a dead germ or virus would enable the body to produce antibodies to give immunity to the disease. The B.C.G. vaccine against tuberculosis (T.B.) was introduced in the early fifties. About the same time, the Salk vaccine, which immunised against poliomyelitis, was discovered.

It was also discovered that if antibodies taken from an immune person were injected into a sick person, they helped him to fight the disease.

Anti-toxins

Even though diagnosis improved and immunisation helped to prevent sickness, there was still the problem of producing medicines which would fight disease. Experiments were carried out to find drugs to fight the toxins or poisons introduced into the body by germs. These drugs were called 'anti-toxins'.

Paul Ehrlich, a Jew, discovered that germs were attracted to certain dyes. He also found that some dyes stained only one kind of tissue in the body. He realised that these dyes could be used to kill germs inside the body by carrying a drug to an exact part of the body. In 1910 he discovered 'Salvarsan' or '606', the first wonder drug.

In 1935 Gerhard Domagk, a German, discovered that the dye, 'Prontosil red', gave protection against streptococci, bacteria which can cause infection. The sulfa drugs, developed from this dye, cured a wide variety of disease, including meningitis.

Antibiotics

In 1928 Sir Alexander Fleming discovered the first 'antibiotic', penicillin. While anti-toxins only prevented the germs from multiplying, an antibiotic actually killed the germs. Fleming noticed that some mould which had accidentally blown into a culture dish containing germs, seemed to be killing them. Although Fleming realised the value of his discovery he could find no way of producing large quantities of penicillin. Ten years later an Australian, Howard Florey, and a German, Ernst Chain, read of Fleming's work and succeeded in finding a way to produce penicillin quickly.

Many more antibiotics have been discovered and new drugs appear almost every day. As drugs are developed, so, unfortunately, the germs develop a resistance to them. Large firms in the drug industry spend a great deal of money on research to find new germ-killers.

A modern research laboratory

Sir Alexander Fleming

29

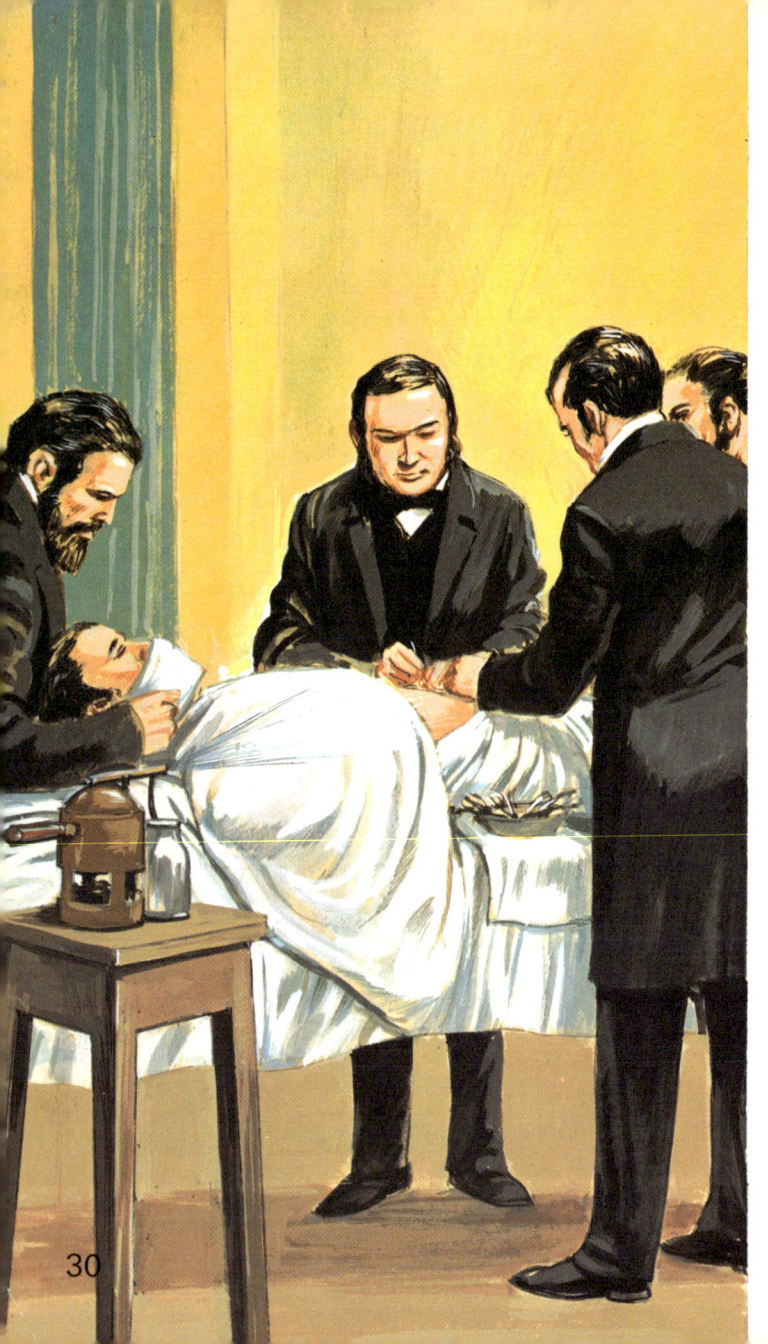

Surgery

Some illnesses can be cured with medicine but others require an operation. At the beginning of the nineteenth century it was said that a soldier on the battlefield was more likely to stay alive than a patient having an operation. This was because of the danger to the patient of blood-poisoning from germs and the shock of having an operation without the help of any pain-killers.

Joseph Lister

During the 1860's Joseph Lister, a surgeon from Glasgow, was worried about the infection which killed patients after surgery. He read of Pasteur's work and realised that germs could be carried on clothing, hands, instruments, dressings, and in the air. He introduced an 'antiseptic' treatment, in which everything coming into contact with the patient was treated with weak carbolic acid to kill the germs. By 1870 he was using a hand-operated carbolic spray so that the acid was also sprayed in the air above the patient. His success was remarkable.

Lister's spray in use during an operation

Asepsis

A Hungarian, Ignaz Semmelweis, and Oliver Wendell Holmes, an American, noticed that women who had babies were more likely to get blood-poisoning if they were attended by medical students or doctors than if they were treated by midwives. These two doctors realised that students and doctors often went straight to the women after treating people with an infectious disease. As they never changed their clothes or washed their hands between visits, they were, in fact, dangerous germ-carriers. By washing their hands they reduced the spread of infection. This was known as the 'aseptic' system, which meant that keeping harmful germs away was better than having to kill them.

By 1886 sterilisation, using steam, was a common practice, and surgeons began wearing gowns, masks and caps. An American surgeon in 1890 took the precaution of using thin rubber gloves.

Today every precaution is taken to keep germs out of the operating theatre. Only sterilised instruments touch the patient and all garments worn are sterilised. The operating theatres are designed so that there are no ledges or crevices where dust can collect. Even a person with a mild cold is excluded from the theatre.

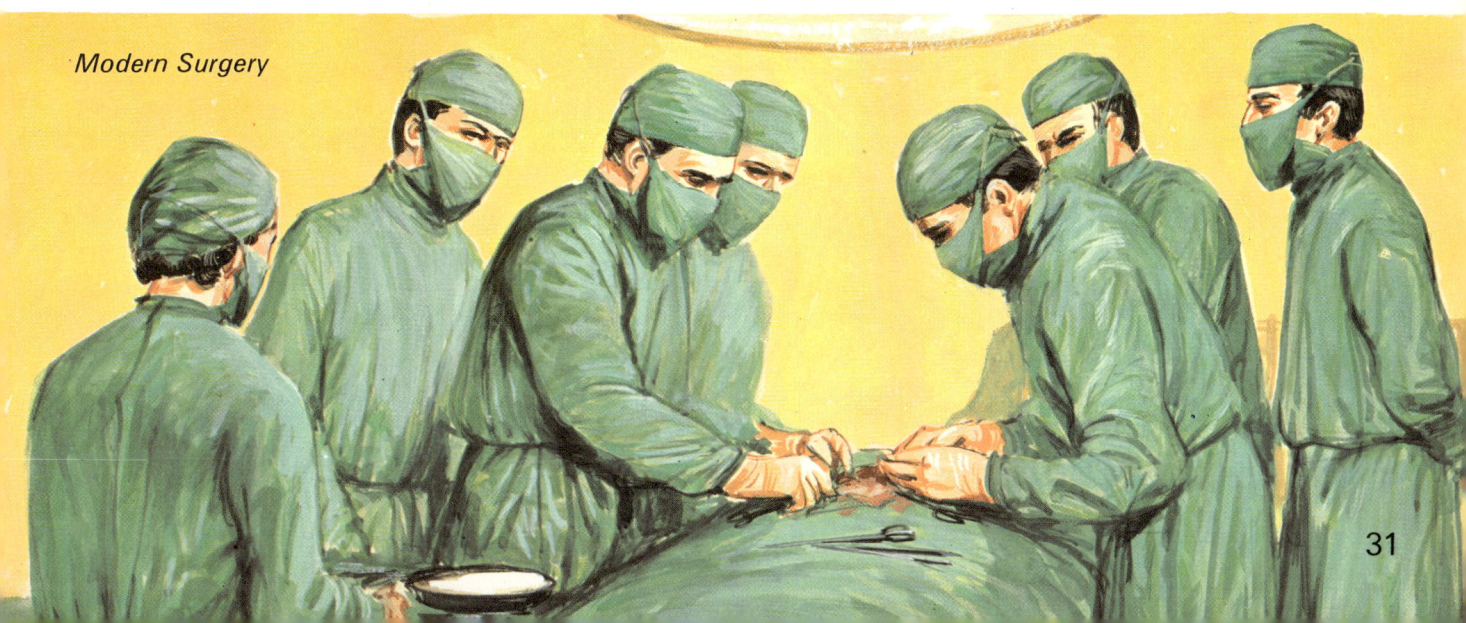

Modern Surgery

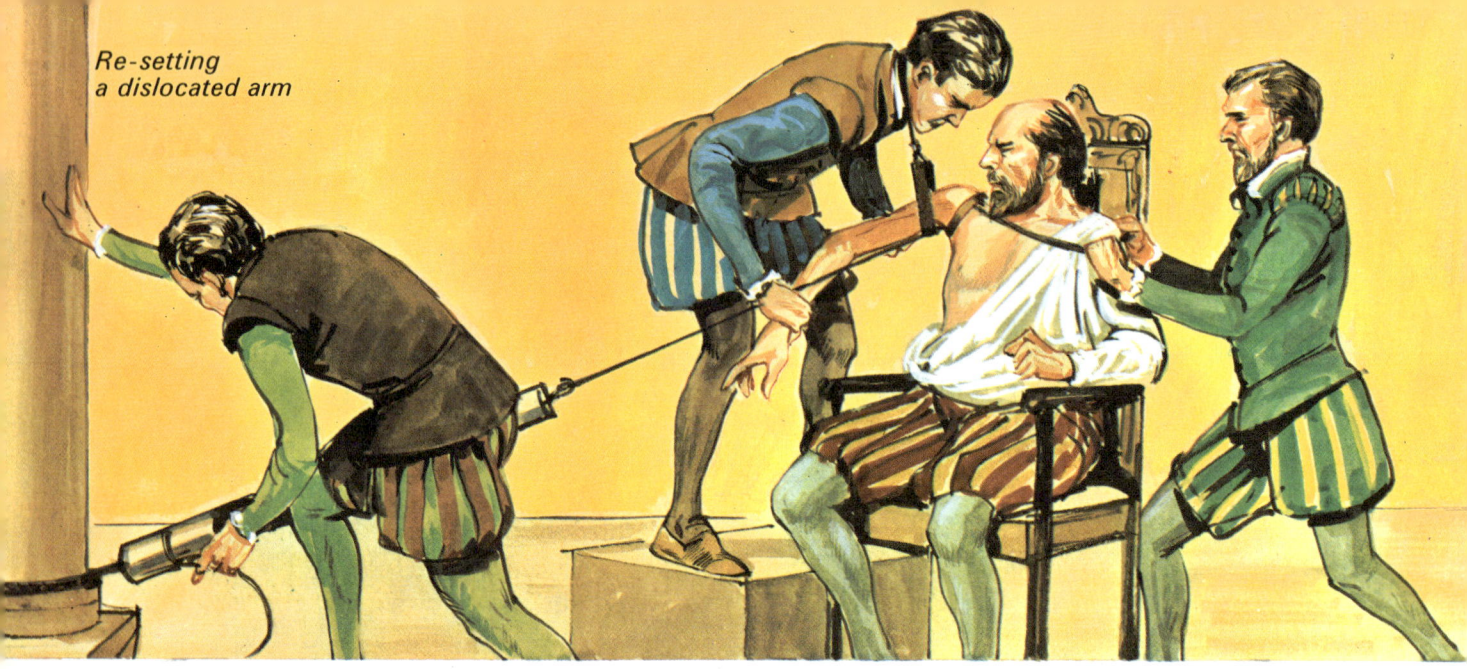

Re-setting a dislocated arm

Killing Pain

Until the nineteenth century there was no known method of putting a patient to sleep for an operation. Pain-killers, such as opium and mandragora which had been known in the Ancient World had been forgotten.

In the nineteenth century a patient could be made drunk, or sometimes a clamp was used to stop blood circulation. Hypnosis was tried, or ice was put on the body to freeze it to kill the pain. Usually, a patient was held down while the surgeon did his work.

In 1799 Sir Humphry Davy published details of his experiments with a gas called 'nitrous oxide' which he had used to put himself and his friends to sleep. His work, however, was ignored at the time. In 1838 Michael Faraday showed that when ether was inhaled it had the same sleep-producing effect. It became a silly joke at parties to inhale ether.

A group of young Americans noticed that after inhaling ether they could not recollect falling, though they had bruises on their bodies. In 1842 one of these men,

Crawford Long, put a patient to sleep, using a towel soaked in ether, and then performed an operation. In 1844 Horace Wells, another American, began to use nitrous oxide in his dentistry work. He gave a public demonstration in 1845, but unfortunately the patient groaned and he failed to convince people of the safety of his method.

On 16th October 1846 William Morton performed a successful operation using ether, assisted by a well-known surgeon, John Warren.

Chloroform

Meanwhile Sir James Simpson, a professor of midwifery at Edinburgh, tried chloroform on women during childbirth. This proved so successful that chloroform replaced ether in general surgery.

Strange to say, the Church fought the use of anaesthetics during childbirth. In 1853 chloroform was used when Queen Victoria had her seventh child. Her doctor, Dr. John Snow, became the first professional anaesthetist, that is, a doctor skilled in the use of anaesthetics. He gave chloroform scientifically, taking into account the weight of blood in a patient. He developed an inhaler so that 'he could mix air with the gas and control its strength.

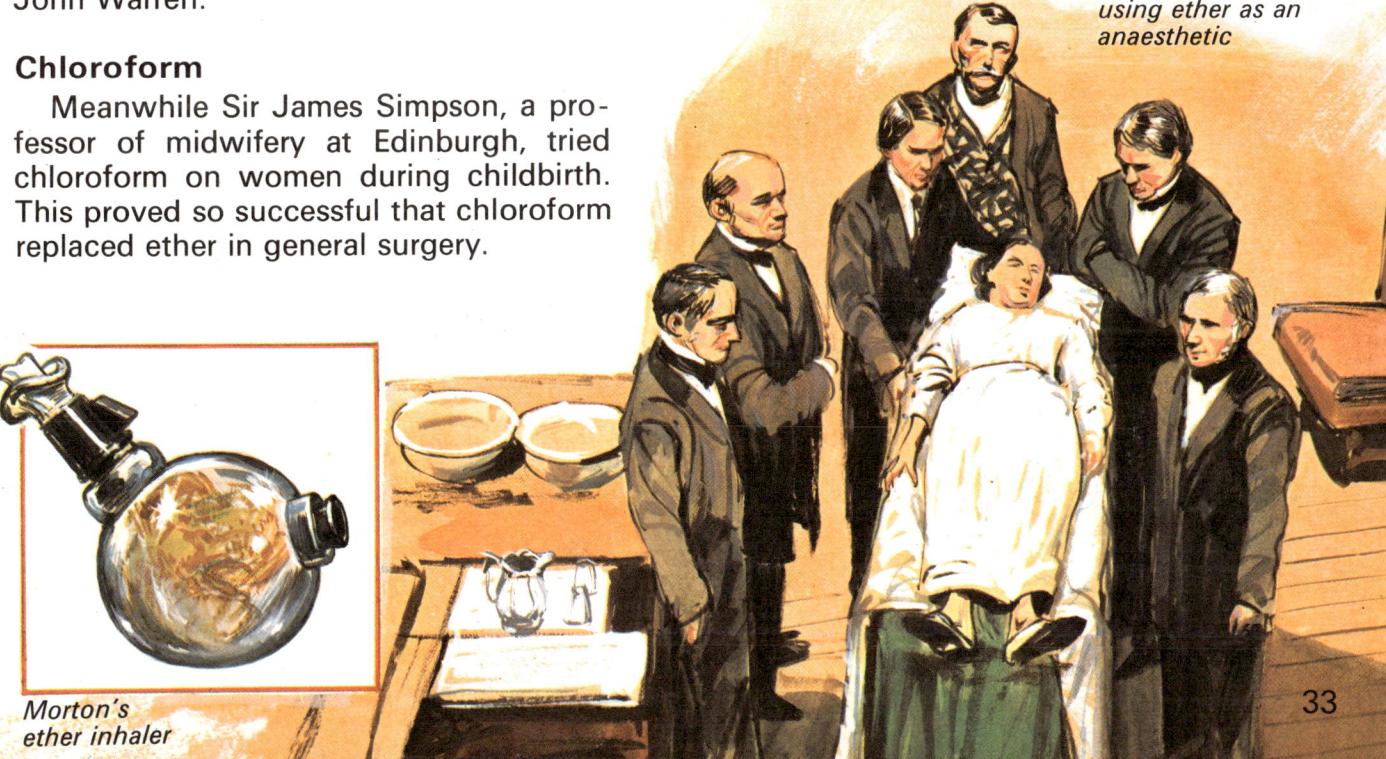

An early operation using ether as an anaesthetic

Morton's ether inhaler

33

In 1903 a patient was put to sleep by injecting a 'barbiturate' into the arm. This enabled the patient to go to sleep without the need of a mask over the face. However, when a barbiturate was used the muscles of the body remained tense, so by 1932 both a barbiturate and an anaesthetic gas were used. In 1945 it was found that when the drug 'curare' was injected, it relaxed the muscles and so less gas was needed.

Anaesthetics Today

The anaesthetist is a highly-qualified doctor who uses a wide range of drugs, and his equipment is very different from that of his forerunners. When patients were breathing vapour from a rag soaked in fluid it was not known how much they were inhaling. Today the gas is in a cylinder, with flexible tubing leading to a face mask. Dials show the exact amount of gas given. A special tube called the 'airway' is placed in the mouth to keep a passage to the lungs clear. For operations on the face and head a special type of tube is used which makes a mask unnecessary.

With the patient comfortably asleep much more complicated surgery is possible.

A modern anaesthetist

Local Anaesthetics

A patient is put to sleep by a general anaesthetic — but a 'general' is not always needed. In 1860 a German chemist extracted the drug 'cocaine' from the coca plant, found in Peru. When this drug, which is a local anaesthetic, was injected into a part of the body, that part became numb and no pain could be felt there. In 1883 cocaine was used to perform a successful eye operation. Cocaine is specially useful for dentists who wish to fill or extract teeth.

In 1898 August Bier of Berlin proved that when cocaine was injected into the spine, the body was numb below the point of injection and so this part could be operated on. Today we have procaine, nupercaine and amethocaine, which produce the same effect on the body, but they are better than cocaine, because they are not habit-forming.

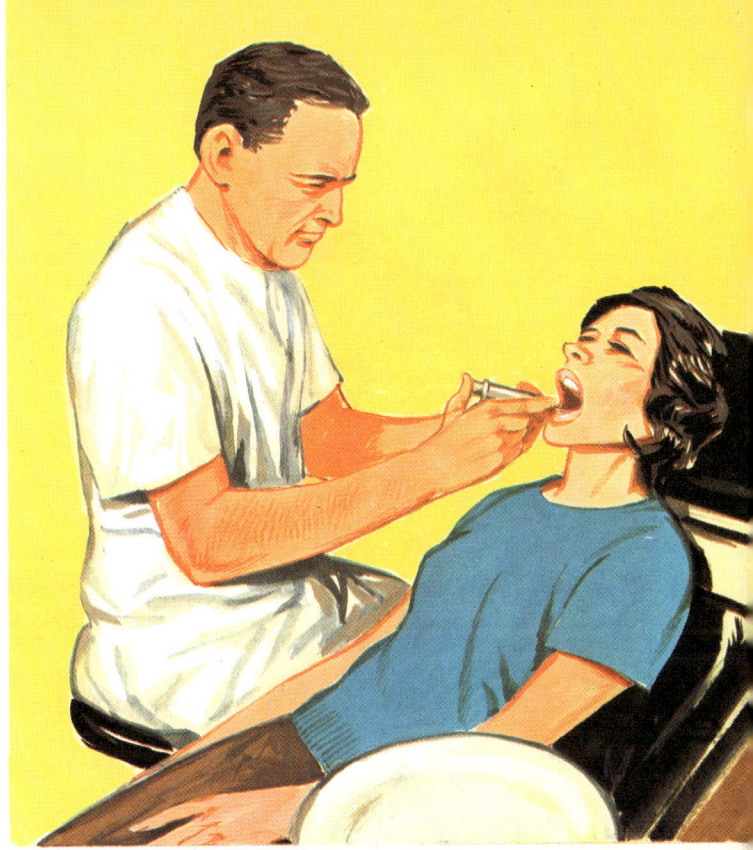

A hypodermic syringe

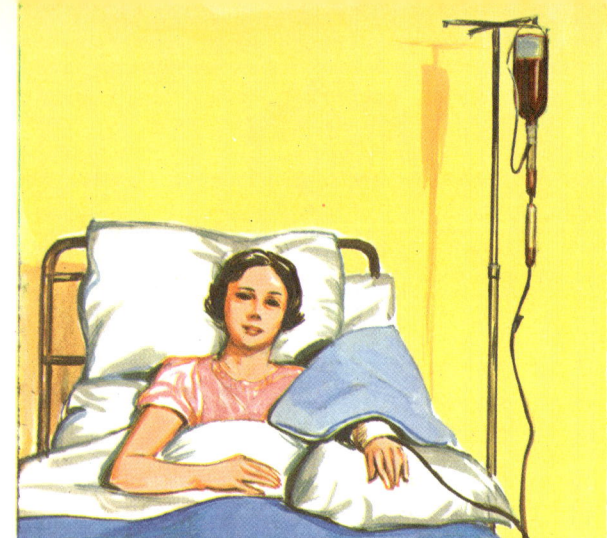

special rays which passed through the tissue of the body but did not pass through bone or metal. He called these 'X-rays'. With an X-ray machine the operator could photograph the bone structure of the body. Early X-ray machines took up to half an hour to obtain a photograph, but a modern machine takes a photograph in seconds. Later it was discovered that if a patient drank a solution of barium sulphate, or was given an injection of other substances, photographs of internal organs could also be taken.

Blood-Transfusions

In 1818, in London, Doctor James Blundell successfully gave a patient a transfusion of blood from another person, and in 1829 a blood-transfusion saved a woman's life. However, there were many failures until doctors realised that there were different types of blood which did not mix. It was discovered in 1910 that there were four main blood groups and since then blood-transfusions have saved many lives. Today blood can be stored in 'blood banks' ready for immediate use.

X-Rays

Until 1895 the surgeon could only guess what a person's internal injuries were. Then Wilhelm Röntgen discovered

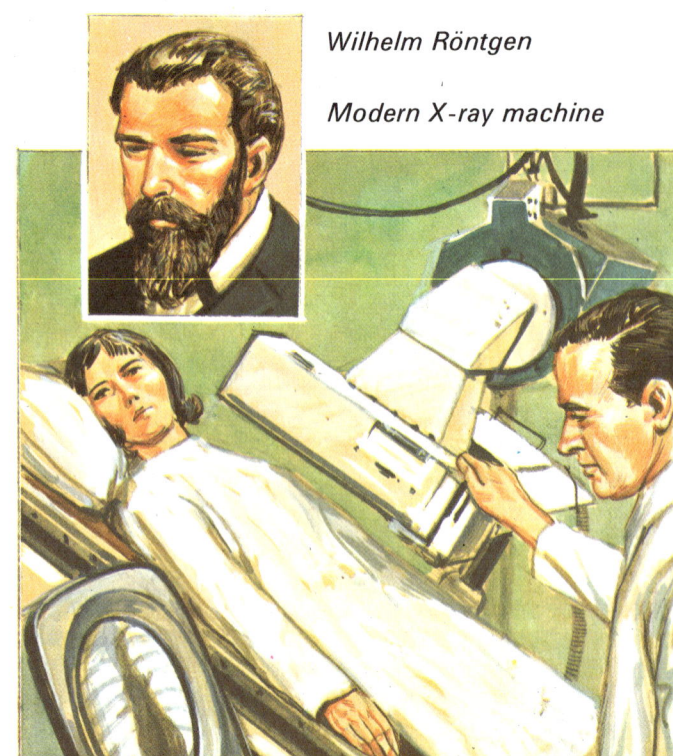

Wilhelm Röntgen

Modern X-ray machine

Marie and Pierre Curie

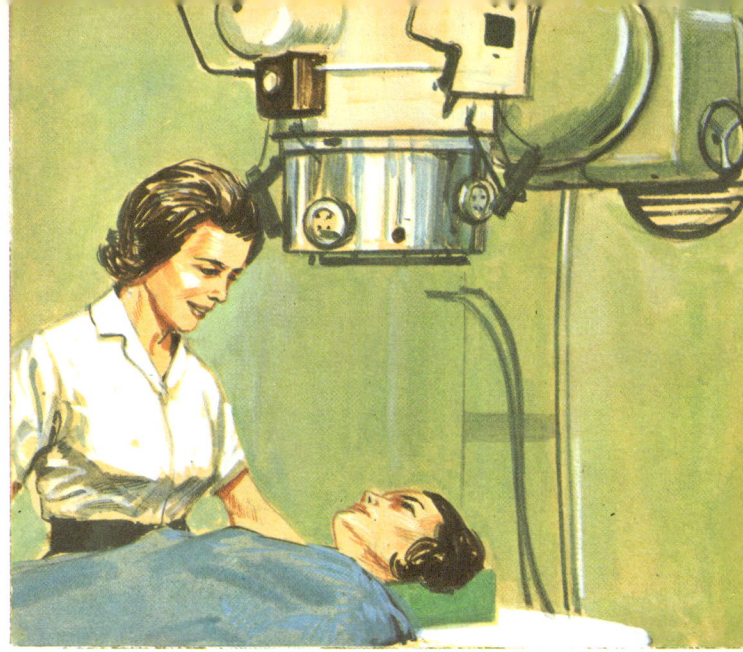

Cobalt-60 machine

Marie and Pierre Curie

Marie and Pierre Curie discovered another source of these X-rays when they isolated radium and polonium in 1902. Radium was used to fight cancer.

Today 'cobalt-60', which is produced by nuclear reactors, is used instead of radium.

Advanced Surgery

An operation on an internal organ was difficult to perform, as each organ of the body needs a constant supply of oxygen which is carried in the blood stream. It was discovered that when the body temperature was reduced less oxygen was required. Using drugs, and a special cooling blanket, or by passing the blood through a cooling machine, the circulation can be safely stopped for up to ten minutes.

Artificial Organs

During the Second World War Doctor Willem Kolff developed an artificial kidney. In 1954 at Hammersmith Hospital, London, a heart-lung machine was introduced which enabled surgeons to perform more difficult operations on the heart.

'Spare Parts'

Since 1945 it has been found possible to transfer certain tissues, such as the cornea of the eye, from one patient to another. There have even been transplants of kidneys and hearts, though with only limited success.

By keeping spare parts in deep freeze, it may be possible in the future to keep a store of organs of the body which the surgeon can use to replace worn-out parts in an otherwise healthy person.

Plastic Surgery

Surgeons today are able to take pieces of skin, bone, muscle or fat from one part of the body and transfer them to another part which may have been badly injured. Skin-grafting and plastic surgery were pioneered by Harold Gillies from New Zealand. During the Second World War, many servicemen had reason to be very grateful for plastic surgery.

Mental Illness

There was little advance during the nineteenth century in the treatment of mental illness. A new form of treatment was pioneered by Sigmund Freud and Carl Jung. It was called 'psycho-analysis', and benefited some patients. However, locked cells, padded cells and strait jackets were still in use at most mental hospitals. Some doctors believed in the 'open door' treatment where patients were free to roam about inside the hospital building, but this has been carried out during the twentieth century only where mood-changing drugs and tranquillizers formed part of the treatment.

During the 1920's the 'electro-encephalograph' (E.E.G.) was developed. This machine could detect brain damage, and in the late 1930's 'electro-convulsive therapy', in which shock waves were sent to the brain by using electricity, was practised.

Today, many people who enter mental hospitals can be cured. When the patients leave hospital Mental Welfare Officers help them to get back to a normal life.

Strait jacket, 1830

Patient prepared for electro-convulsive therapy

39

Welfare clinic

District nurse

Government Control
Public Health

The poor living conditions of the working class in Britain in the nineteenth century made the problem of disease more serious. Crowded living quarters with polluted water, a lack of sewers, poor diets, and long working hours caused much sickness and ill-health.

The Public Health Acts of 1848 and 1875 tried to remedy this. Local Authorities were made responsible for the welfare of people. They controlled all building and were expected to provide proper sewage and waste disposal.

Medical Officers of Health were appointed. Medical inspection of schools began in 1907, and the Ministry of Health was established in 1918. During the twentieth century district nurses, health visitors, home nurses and midwives were appointed.

Infant Welfare Centres were opened. As it was known that the body needed certain chemicals, called 'vitamins', there was stricter supervision of food.

Great care is now taken to see that nursing mothers and young children receive enough of these essential vitamins.

Since the first Clean Air Act of 1956 there is control over the air we breathe.

Mental Care

In 1808 an Act of Parliament gave Local Authorities the power to build asylums out of the rates. A later Act of 1845 made the building of asylums compulsory, and they all had to be regularly inspected. From 1889 they were controlled by County Councils. After the Mental Treatment Act of 1930 patients could go into mental hospitals for treatment of their own free will.

In 1946 all mental hospitals came under the control of the National Health Service.

Hospitals

During the nineteenth century there was a lack of hospitals. In 1929 County Councils were given the power to turn work-houses into hospitals, and to do this they were helped by a government grant.

By 1939 Municipal and Voluntary hospitals existed side by side in most areas.

After the National Health Service Act of 1946 most hospitals were under state control. The country was divided into regions, each of which had teaching hospitals, and general and special hospitals.

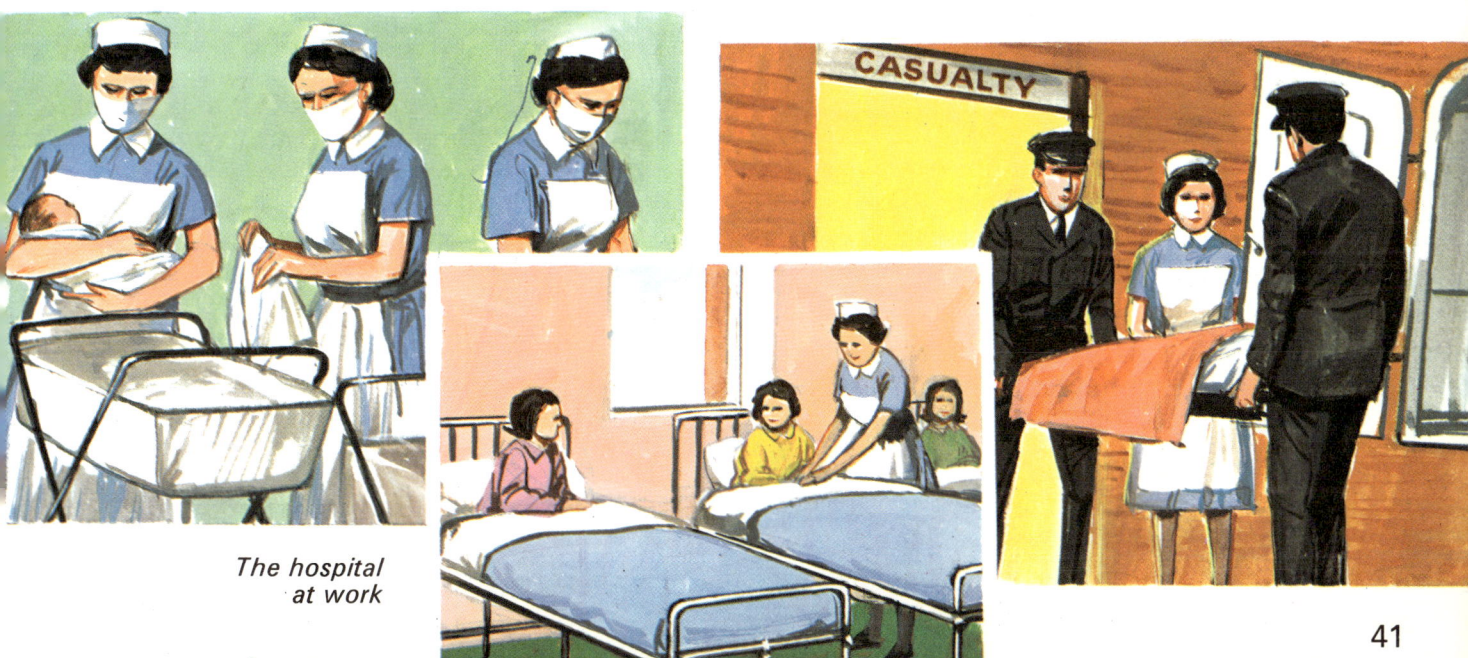

The hospital at work

The tremendous progress which medicine has made during the nineteenth and twentieth centuries would have been impossible without better nurses and doctors.

Nursing

The typical nurse at the beginning of the nineteenth century was ill-trained and slovenly. She wore no uniform, was paid little money, and was expected to cook her own food. She could not even be relied upon to carry out a doctor's instructions. Some attempt was made to improve the quality of nursing. The Church of England founded an order of nursing nuns in 1848. These nurses received training. They worked for two years as probationers and then did five years' work in a hospital before they were given a certificate.

Florence Nightingale

Florence Nightingale worked very hard to raise the standard of nursing. She visited the Institute of Kaiserswerth in Germany, controlled by Pastor Theodor Fliedner, and was very impressed by the first-class nursing of the deaconesses there.

The Florence Nightingale
School of Nursing

A modern nursing school

She was given a chance to show her nursing skill when she was invited to go out to the Crimea to reorganise the nursing of the wounded soldiers. So successful was she that grateful people in Britain gave over £44,000 as a testimonial to her. She decided to use the money to set up the Florence Nightingale School of Nursing at St. Thomas's Hospital in London.

The first fifteen student nurses were carefully chosen and began their training in July 1860. They wore uniforms and their training was carefully supervised.

When not on duty they lived in a nurses' home. They received one year's training and then had two years' supervised work on the staff of the hospital.

Other hospitals set up teaching hospitals and often Nightingale nurses were invited to direct the training. At last, hospitals now had trained medical nurses and nursing was looked upon as a profession.

Today a nurse has to have a great deal of medical knowledge so that she can carry out her duties well and give more help to the doctors.

Doctors

Doctors have reached a higher standard in their profession. This is because they have more effective drugs, the advantage of new developments, and, most important, they are better trained.

After the Apothecaries Act of 1815 doctors had to pass examinations in order to qualify fully. The trainee was apprenticed to an apothecary, and had to attend a course of lectures and have experience in hospital work. Soon private medical schools were opened to prepare students for their examinations. These were gradu-ally taken over by the medical schools attached to the hospitals, and later by the universities. Each hospital, however, set its own examinations and there was a great difference in the standards expected. By the Medical Act of 1858 more uniform standards were established. A General Council of Medical Education and Regis-tration (later called the General Medical Council) was set up with a register of qualified doctors. The Council supervised the training and conduct of members and had the right to discipline them.

Instruction in a 19th-century medical school

44

Students watching an operation on close-circuit TV

Unqualified doctors could still practise medicine but they could not use the title of 'doctor'. Only a registered doctor could sign a death certificate and prescribe or keep dangerous drugs.

Some doctors become 'general practitioners' (G.P.s). They live in the community and attend to the medical needs of the people around them. Others join the staff of the hospitals to become specialists in one particular type of medical care, and some work as consultants at the hospitals.

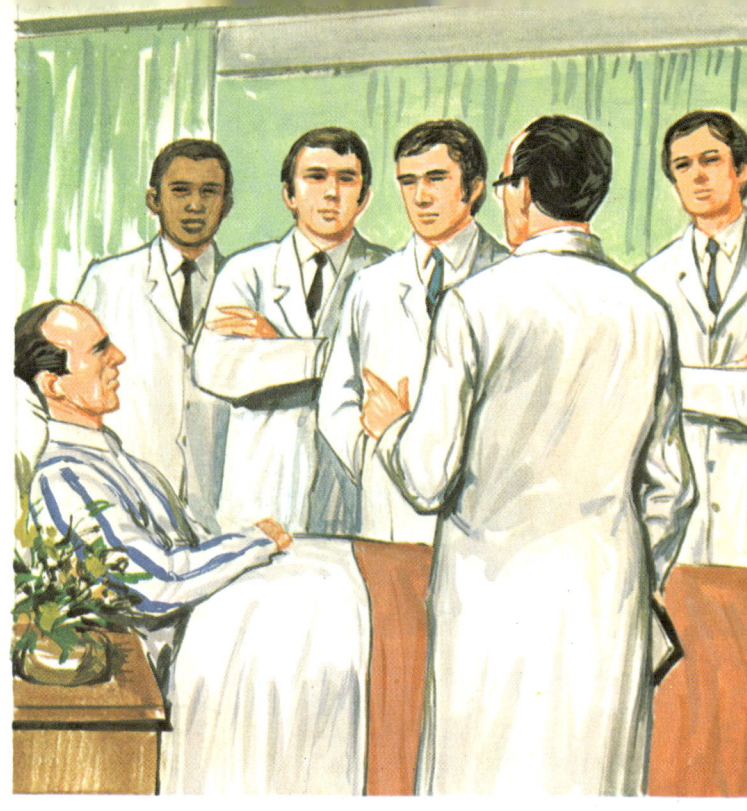

Students accompanying a consultant on his rounds

The G.P. no longer works alone. He keeps in close touch with the doctors and specialists in the hospitals. Ambulances, helicopters and even light aircraft are ready to rush people to hospital in case of accident or dangerous illness. There is a steady flow of people sent by their doctors to the hospitals for tests, X-rays, and consultations.

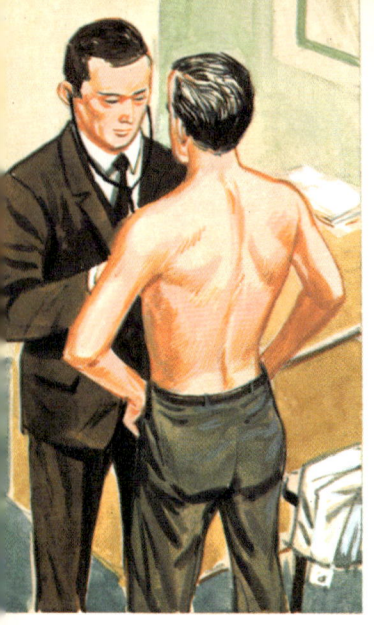

The National Health Service

Until 1946 medical treatment had to be paid for by the patient. He paid a fee to his doctor and bought the drugs prescribed. Treatment, other than that received in a voluntary hospital or an infirmary, also had to be paid for. Doctors employed debt collectors to collect fees. Poor people often did not have a doctor as they were unable to pay the necessary fees.

An Insurance Act of 1911 compelled workers and employers to pay a small amount of money each week so that if a man were sick he could receive sick pay and free medical treatment. The treatment, however, was not yet free for his wife or children.

The National Health Service Act of 1946 said that most medical treatment should be free: doctors, hospitals, drugs, spectacles, and even hearing aids. In July 1948 the Government began providing free dental treatment. The money for the health service in Britain comes directly from taxation. Since 1948 the cost of the Service has steadily increased and people are expected to pay a contribution towards the cost of the drugs and treatment. Old people, children and the very poor still receive all treatment free.

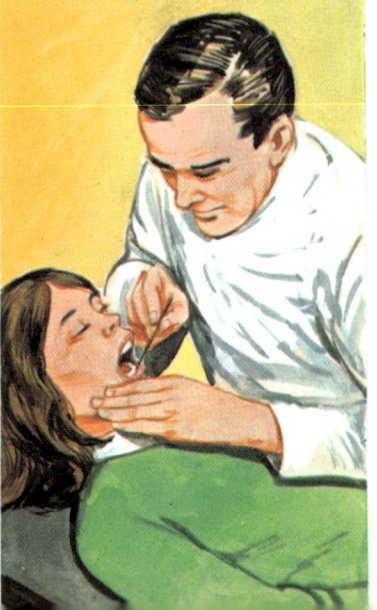

Red Cross workers

W.H.O. badge

World Health

Today disease travels with alarming speed. The World Health Organisation was formed in 1948. It links together all forms of medical research and receives reports of serious outbreaks of disease. International teams go out to fight malaria, leprosy and other outbreaks of infectious diseases. News of epidemics is sent to the headquarters in Geneva. Medical officers are quickly informed and suspected cases from danger areas are taken to hospital.

The W.H.O. rushes help to areas stricken with disasters like earthquakes, hurricanes, and large scale epidemics. The Red Cross, founded in 1864 on the advice of Jean Henri Dunant, gives valuable assistance in this work.

The W.H.O. also sends out international nurses to teach people in developing countries how to care for the sick.

A World-Wide Service

Today, most people have trained medical service within their reach. Fishing fleets often take with them a hospital ship. Doctors and nurses use aircraft, snowmobiles, jeeps, and even elephants, to reach people in need of help. Services like the 'Flying Doctor' ensure that those needing hospital care can obtain it quickly. Medicine has become a world-wide service.

INDEX